MW01223893

¡WORD UP!

Hope For Youth Poetry From El Centro De La Raza

Edited By Zoë Anglesey

¡WORD UP!

Hope For Youth Poetry
from El Centro de la Raza

ISBN: 0-9633275-1-8
Library of Congress Catalog Card Number: 92-090571

Manufactured in the United States of America

FOR INFORMATION WRITE:

Roy D. Wilson
Director
Department of Community Outreach
and International Relations
El Centro de la Raza
2524 16th Avenue South
Seattle, WA 98144
Phone: 206-329-2974
Fax: 206-329-0786

ACKNOWLEDGMENTS

We are grateful for permission to include in ¡WORD UP! the following:

"Get Ready" by Rebecca Inéz Bockelie, originally published in: Judith A. Billings, "Superintendent's Message," *Education News*, Olympia Washington, September 1991; and as a broadside by Louis Collins of Louis Collins Books, Seattle.

"Parrots" and "Vision from a Little Blue Window" by Ernesto Cardenal appear in *Flights of Victory/Vuelos de Victoria*, edited and translated by Marc Zimmerman, (Curbstone Press, Willimantic, CT, 1985).

"Equal to a Pebble" by Roberto Obregón is from *El Fuego Perdido*, translation by Zoë Anglesey.

"Ars Poetica" by Mirna Martínez appears in Ixok *Amar.go: Central American Women's Poetry for Peace*, Ed., Zoë Anglesey, (Granite Press, 1987), translation by Zoë Anglesey.

"Cenote" by Monica Mansour is originally from *Con La Vida Al Hombre*. This bilingual poem appears in *Mouth to Mouth: Twelve Contemporary Mexican Women Poets,* edited by Forrest Gander (Milkweed Editions, 1983).

EL CENTRO DE LA RAZA

Assistant to Roy D. Wilson:
Debra Ross
Hope for Youth Program Directors:
Melissa Lopez, Fatima Bucsit
Hope for Youth Art Teacher:
Fulgencio Lazo-Amaya
Art Workshop Assistants:
Santiago Olguin, Victor Bojorquez, Oscar Williams, Tracy
Tsutsumuto, Sarah Moore, Juan Piña, Hilda Rosaura O'Leary

Editor and Poetry Workshop Teacher:
Zoë Anglesey
Workshop Assistants:
Cynthia Contreras Bockelie, Hap Bockelie, Peter James,
Margaret O'Donnell, Antonio Maestas, Miguel Maestas,
Marlene Mersch, Alex McGee, Eva Pannabecker, Steve
Toutonghi, Barbara Wiley, Michele Williams
Workshop Translators:
Karen Bohlke, Erin Fanning, Miguel Maestas, Marlene Mersch,
Juan Piña, Debra Ross, Maria Agduyeng, Brenda Agduyeng
Tagalog Translator: Lourdes Verzosa

Cover Art: Armando Martinez, *Hermiston Melon For Lunch*,
(Serigraph, tempera on paper, 8" x 11")
Book Design: Anglesey, Toutonghi, Reavis
Publicity, Design and Production Consultant: Sally B. Reavis
Desktop Publishing: Steve Toutonghi
Printer: Allied Printers, Seattle WA
Photograph of Hope For Youth Students: Gil Reavis
Photograph of Hope For Youth Members with Ernesto
Cardenal, August 1991: Diane Passmore

Special thanks also to Aldus Corporation for the donation of
computer time and expertise toward the making of
¡WORD UP!

This book was designed and produced using Aldus Freehand®, Aldus
PageMaker®, Aldus PrePrint®, and Aldus® PressWise™ for the Apple®
Macintosh®. It was typeset in Gill Sans 10/12.

DEDICATION

Creo que todo ser humano es poeta, como todo pájaro canta, y así también lo creía Goethe. Y esto está confirmado una vez más con los poemas de niños y niñas del Taller de Poesía de la comunidad hispana de Seattle oganizado por el Centro de la Raza. Todo ser humano es poeta pero en la mayoría la poesía se atrofia por falta de orientacíon. Esa es la gran importancia de los Talleres de Poesía, en Seattle como en Nicaragua o en cualquier otra parte. En todas partes debería haber Talleres de Poesía. Lo demuestra este taller creado recientemente en Seattle. Un gran abrazo a todos.

Ernesto Cardenal

I think that everyone, being human, is a poet, like all birds sing, and as Goethe believed. Here it is confirmed one more time by poems from the Hope For Youth Poetry Workshop. Everyone, being human, is a poet, but most poetry atrophies for lack of direction. Purpose is of utmost importance to the poetry workshops in Seattle, as in Nicaragua or wherever. There should be poetry workshops everywhere. This is demonstrated by the workshop recently established by El Centro de la Raza. A big hug for everyone.

Ernesto Cardenal

PREFACE

Poetry and art have been stolen from our people. Today, among the people of the United States, poetry means practically nothing. Some tolerate it as a private act; others see it as wimpy or not strong. The truth is, poetry, like all forms of art, express values and principles characteristic of a particular class, ethnic group or culture. Poetry, for our children, is one more method of building community and generating power. It is more than a voice, it is the act of being one among others of our community.

El Centro de la Raza, a Chicano-Latino civil rights organization, takes pride in the young people who have produced these poems. They are part of the Hope for Youth Program which promotes service as its fundamental activity. As Dr. Martin Luther King, Jr. has said, everyone can be great because everyone can serve. Hope for Youth develops projects serving our seniors, children and families. The Program also produces many of the cultural/educational events for our organization, including our art and poetry classes.

Each of us who have worked with these young people know that we must bring poetry back to caring people. Poetry workshops have to be one of the least expensive empowerment methods available to those who care about changing the world we live in. Our nation needs a lot of "care" now. Our people face a moral, economic and political crisis. It may sound far-fetched or abstract, but just as we need to bring back the trees and the salmon, we need to bring back poetry. Just as we need to bring back the unions and voter participation, we need to bring back the revolutionary character, the sisterhood and brotherhood of the United States. Just as we need recycled resources or clean air and water now and for the future, we need healthy hearts and minds. As we go about working on these changes, poetry will once again find its place in the lives of the caring people of our nation.

The Hope for Youth Poetry Workshops exist due in large part to Father Ernesto Cardenal and the compañeros from

Solentiname, Nicaragua. Father Cardenal and the Nicaraguan Revolution established nation-wide poetry workshops in the 1980's. It was Father Cardenal who revealed to us that poetry was, all along, a part of the lives of caring people, and that we must all do our part to recapture the act of making poems in the community. A special thanks to Father Cardenal who consulted with us, inspired and pointed us along the way.

A special thanks to Rev. Jesse L. Jackson who has done as much as anybody to bring poetry back to main street and my street! Rev. Jackson's organizing methods and empowering guidance have assisted us in understanding and in doing our work.

Special thanks to the teacher, Zoë Anglesey, who knows how to trigger love and energy in others and has the skill to channel it into success.

The poems speak for themselves. So do the youth. We simply ask that you respond to these poems by these young people who have expressed their caring. This book is an invitation. If in reading ¡WORD UP! you discover someone whom you'd like to know better, please respond. One thing is certain: poetry and caring people used to be one and the same thing in our nation. It's coming back. This thing is not going away.

Roy D. Wilson
April, 1992

INTRODUCTION

ORIGINS OF THE EL CENTRO DE LA RAZA HOPE FOR YOUTH POETRY WORKSHOPS

I am reminded of the WPA's Federal Arts Projects during the Great Depression which employed some of this country's great writers. In spite of the current "recession," El Centro de la Raza found the means to sponsor free poetry workshops thanks to conscientious donors. Many of my colleagues from the time when we were CETA poets in the late 1970s are now renowned "performance poets." Their influence stamps the video *Words In Your Face* which I show to the Hope for Youth students. They see young poets truly being themselves with whom they can identify. I also applied a variety of techniques emerging constantly from the poetry workshop movement across this country that spans from St. Marks Church-on-the-Bowery to Centrum at Fort Worden State Park in Port Townsend. My participation in the *Taller de los Lunes* (Monday Workshops) in Costa Rica and the *talleres* that created the chapbooks, *Poesía Libre,* in Sandinista Nicaragua (started by Ernesto Cardenal) provide ongoing guidance for our workshops at El Centro de la Raza.

Invited as a participating poet to the Rubén Darío Poetry Festival, I was in Bluefields, Nicaragua on the Caribbean coast in January 1986 when I met Roy Wilson with Seattle's Total Experience Gospel Choir. On this trip I was privileged to accompany Allen Ginsberg, the great "Beat" poet. We read our poetry in noon-blazing plazas and patios. We heard the poets of Bluefields read in libraries and candle-lit rooms. During this interchange, nothing was lost in the translation! In fact that was my purpose in Central America these years: to bring back poetry letting the people of Central America speak for themselves through those who are most expressive and articulate—their poets. This same concept functioned in the Hope For Youth workshops—let the youth speak for themselves. Sometimes that requires translation from the Spanish or Tagalog. Simultaneous translation in Spanish is always available from the staff at El Centro de la Raza. The translations in this book, if they reach the level of poetry in English compared to the original in Spanish, are not literal, but literary. Years of translating poetry as well as reading translations by the exemplary likes of Gregory Rebassa establish the precedence.

THE WORKSHOPS

The goals of El Centro de la Raza are implemented in the Hope For Youth poetry workshops. The young authors in this anthology show evidence of pride in their heritages and selves. Besides writing poems, the workshops are meant to realize empowerment, leadership, and self-discipline. This is not easy rhetoric. When young people see their thoughts transcribed to text on a page, they feel a sense of accomplishment which is also satisfying to families, peers and the mentors who surround them at El Centro de la Raza. When they read their poetry through a microphone, which we practice to better enunciate and project feeling and meaning, these young people merit the applause they receive. This makes them feel proud.

Writing poetry puts the child in contact with the creative process and at the same time introduces them to the art of poetry itself. Pedagogically speaking, they practice writing and cognitive skills. They learn to choose a language that corresponds to their emerging value system. Throughout the workshop they are introduced to poetry by wondrous poets from various cultures writing in diverse languages. Presentation of a poem from the Caribbean or Central America requires going to a map, explaining terminology or idioms and providing a context. Indirectly, then, they learn something of the history and geography of a poem, which is as important as the language it is written in.

Integral to the workshop is the critical but supportive discussion to increase a poem's impact. Analyzing elements of a poem can also lead to a host of interdisciplinary understandings. The workshop teaches specific skills and whether or not the students wish to dedicate their lives to poetry, the self-discipline that writing requires empowers them.

With students seated at tables arranged in a circle, the two-hour sessions usually begin with a reading of several contemporary poems. When reading Chicano or Puerto Rican poetry, students are well aware that the majority in the Americas speak Spanish, as does the fastest growing sector of the population in the United States. English and Spanish naturally converge when and where the two cultures intersect, certainly on the streets. Students, therefore, enjoy collaging the two vocabularies which invariably bonds the syntax from both languages.

The interactive process I learned at Boricua College in New York transposes easily to the workshop setting. It requires the following: receiving—listening, focusing, being open to feelings; responding—sharing, discussing, writing, reading aloud, expressing emotions; and valuing—appreciating poetry from others and one's self. Keeping a balance between these three activities makes for an optimal workshop environment.

After students are introduced to a theme or technique, they begin fashioning a poem. Students often take advantage of being able to dictate first drafts to adult assistants. This helps younger students who may not have the speed to write by hand what is spilling from their minds. Because poetry requires an exact, precise vocabulary, assistants also help students use dictionaries, bilingual dictionaries and the thesaurus. At times I put synonyms of words or metaphors derived from discussion on the blackboard so students can, if they wish, select what they need to express their exact idea. When students wrote about the Dance Theater of Harlem's performance, they listed various ways of saying "red" to describe more exactly the colors of the set and costumes. We thought up synonyms for "jump" so as to better express the graceful leaps they admired. This was an opportunity to introduce the particular vocabulary of ballet which extended their initial enjoyment of the dances into a comprehensive, educative experience. In addition, one-on-one assistants probe beyond the idea a student has to stimulate the flow of associations. I look forward to answering questions that let me explain the culture-bound etymology of words. So we do what they did in the Nicaraguan workshops—strengthen the level of literacy.

Because the workshop meets down the hall from the El Centro de la Raza Gallery, students see exhibits regularly. Some workshops are devoted to translating the visual imagery into the verbal for a poem. Several poems in ¡WORD UP! come from transcribing observations of prints or painting. Observation remains a primary prerequisite for writing poetry. This kindles a new respect for the person, object, phenomena or visual work observed. "Charlie's Ghost" by Javier Piña was written with an acute sense of observation which yielded meaningful details that resonate between the lines. This demands more than casual looking. Intense observation requires the discipline of prolonged examination to learn or feel at a new level of awareness.

The poems we share in the workshop serve as example for theme or technique. Ernesto Cardenal's poem "Ecology" (*Flight of Victory*, Curbstone, 1988), sets in motion writing about the environment. Cardenal's poem "Vision from a Small Blue Window" (see page 18) with Mirna Martínez's "Ars Poetica" (*Ixok Amar.Go*, see page 36) written in response to Rubén Darío's *Azul*, prompts ruminations on colors like Sandra Martinez's "Wearing Red" and Armando Martinez's "Black." Roberto Obregón's "Like a Pebble" (see page 111) inspired Veronica Castañeda's "Aguzadera" and Kenia Lewis's "La Palabra." Besides utilizing Richard Hugo's technique of starting with a phrase to trigger associations vital for the content of a poem, reading his poems of place set in the Pacific Northwest inspired the "Ayutla" poems. Among the forms of poetry focused on, the ode is a favorite thanks to Pablo Neruda.

If students write a narrative poem, they learn the technique of culling shiny nouns and stunning verbs of wild shape like they search out agates from common stones. With the findings from this procedure, they arrange a sequence that results in poems like Tierra Greig's "When I Felt Like Running Away," and Eloy Tenorio's "What a Haircut Can Do Unto You." A reader will notice that there are poems about family members, dangers children face, the things children enjoy in particular, and about those abstractions that all poets attempt to write about like love, terms of justice and death.

A NOTE ABOUT CONTEMPORARY POETRY

Contemporary poetry is characterized by a multitude of forms converging within the vast parameters of free verse. Present at the beginning of the Twentieth Century, this poetry rejects strict meters and rhymes to instead trace the rhythms of mind, heart and voice. "Voice" imprints the syntax of a text with what is characteristic of a poet, distinct as one's fingerprints or DNA.

Freedom of expression is another standard within contemporary poetry and relates to the purpose of our workshop. Endangered, the child's unadulterated mind, free from electronic brain-washing, needs to know itself to create. In a society that proclaims freedoms in empty proclamations with lip service to critical thinking and literacy, what in a child's education really encourages free expression of thought or insights? One day Roberto Maestas happened in the workshop as I declared it "liberated territory." That meant without harming others, they were free to write about anything and in any vernacular that was their own. Youth speak a language that sounds like code to adults. Except for honoring the understanding that obscenities have no place at El Centro de la Raza, students could freely write in their young-folks idiom without someone saying it was "bad grammar." Like others at El Centro de la Raza, Roberto Maestas supports the premise by which I made that declaration. Students feel that back-up of support throughout the organization. It should be kept in mind that

that each generation originates ways to set it apart from former generations. This generational process originates a new vocabulary which enriches the language "organically" in a healthy way. The summer 1991/winter 1992 workshops decided that the title of their book should be ¡WORD UP! and so it is.

IN APPRECIATION

This poetry would not be collected had it not been for the wholehearted backing from so many who are involved in the Hope For Youth program. After the workshop sessions, students hear excitement and expectation in the voices of those asking them if they will read their new poems. El Centro de la Raza staff and volunteers, along with parents, give constant encouragement. Students see how their poems fly from notebooks to the copy machine and word processor. This support produces an ambiance that creates honest writing. If poetry does not project true feelings or ideas, what is written will fall within the conventional realm of clichés or sentimentality. I am grateful to the Hope for Youth students for writing memorable poems. I am grateful to their parents who get them to the workshop on time. All of what you read in ¡WORD UP! could not have been written if the youth had been abandoned in front of television sets or on the streets.

Because of the Hope for Youth program we can read poems that reveal what concerns these young people. We can enjoy the humor their intelligence reveals. We may realize there is less of a generation gap than we suspect as we see poems expressing the need for changes in society. We will receive some insights because of whom or what they admire. Their poetry states what matters to them. In the process they reveal something of who they are within the larger community, local and non-local. These poems document their proud selves. They are somebody.

Zoë Anglesey
27 March 1992

CONTENTS

I was born in Tacoma on September 1st, 1981. My parents were born in Los Angeles. I have been coming to El Centro de la Raza since the age of two.

DIEGO BORBOA

EL PERRO

Mira. El perro is eating a burrito
thrown next to that tire of el carro.

A kid says to a tall person
mira el perro with the green collar.

The tall person doesn't watch
how very rapido el perro wants to comer.

GUNS

Guns: They are used to kill and show off
Guns: They make it easy to rip off your money
Guns: They shake in the hand when the person is very angry
Guns: They fit in the pocket for protection
Guns: They give power to gangs
Guns: Their bullets ping shooting cans
Guns: People carry guns cuz they think they're cool
Guns: People kill defenseless animals with guns
Guns: Kids bring guns to school
Guns: I never want to see one stuck in my face

CHANGE AND PAN DULCE

One day I took a walk to the store four blocks away
to buy some pan dulce, pop and a burrito.
On my way I saw two men standing in front of the store
begging for some pesos.
I only had ten dollars.
I said I would come back in five minutes.
When I did I saw them still begging for more pesos.
I only had one dollar in change.
I gave two quarters to one and two quarters to the other
then saving the pop and pan dulce
I walked home eating my burrito.

MY HOLE

I was seven years old
when I dug a hole in my backyard
that led to the neighbor's backyard.

When I was digging
I smelled the rusty smell of dirt.

It took me a month til I was done.
Sometimes my friends would help me.

When I was digging I cut my lip.
Now it looks like lightning.

I crawled up and down that hole everyday.
When I got to my neighbor's house

he gave me good things to eat
like candy.

Born in Seattle on January 19, 1981 on her mother Cynthia Contreras Bockelie's birthday, Marit travels to El Centro de la Raza by ferry from Bremerton with her father Hap Bockelie. She enjoys playing guitar and wants to be a journalist.

MARIT BOCKELIE

RAVEN

There it is, the raven
flapping, cawing, looking out with cautious shiny beads.
It passes over the woods and estuaries
that used to be my great grandmother's land.

The coal-black raven
perches in the cedar tree
grown tall from a tiny seed
that it dropped to earth
where my great grandfather lies buried.

I came.
The raven brought me
to mourn the death of my great grandfather's
cedar tree.

The rich people who only care about themselves
came to build an airport.
They cut down all the cedar
grown from seed
that the raven dropped to earth
where my great grandfather
and others are buried.

Now I sit here
remembering my great grandfather
and the cedar.
I watch the raven
and wonder what will happen next.

STUDYING ALFREDO ARREGUIN'S PAINTING: SACRIFICIO NA AMAZONIA, HONORING FRANCISCO "CHICO" MENDEZ (1944-1988) FROM XAPURI, ACRE IN BRAZIL

Ferns and grasses lie below trees rising like powerful arms
reaching up from the depths of the river.

Two great blue herons hunt quietly through lillipads for fish
fish that mimic every bloom and leaf.

A pair of cobalt macaws pass over the mighty jaguar
its strange twin floats upside down on the rippled inlet.

A monkey swings from deep green vines twisted around the tree
another with a full white beard looks at everything.

In the distant foliage Chico's dark prophetic face
falls on this shadowed habitat ruled by waters.

CLOUDS

The other day, my dad and I were in our car on the ferry.
This afternoon my dad was so tired
he fell asleep.
As he was sleeping, I looked up into the sky
and saw the clouds.

To me the clouds were no different that day
than any other day but I guess I saw them differently.

At first I saw a little bird whose wings were very weak.
She fell beside a small ice-covered pond.
Then I saw a dragon who melted the ice with its breath.
Then the dragon turned into a pig
that had a snout a mile long.
The pig stayed in view for a very very long time.
I blinked and winked to try to get rid of him.
Finally I did.
Maybe something burned him up
or the winds blew him to the Gods.

I saw so many unexplainable things in the sky.
I couldn't understand why I hadn't seen
those wonderful things before.

Now that I've thought about it
one of my favorite pastimes is cloud watching
because it's free.

Anyone and everyone can do it.
It doesn't matter how young, how old
where you come from, what you believe in—
it's free
no matter how rich or poor
wherever you are
it's free.

Born on November 29 1982, Rebecca Inéz's poem has been published in newsletters, journals and as a broadside by rare book dealer Louis Collins. Paul Kantner, formerly with the Jefferson Airplane and now with Starship has recited "Get Ready." She reads "one big book everyday."

REBECCA INÉZ BOCKELIE

LOS COLORES

Rojo dances in flesh and blood
Azul runs clear as agua pura
Verde rustles like a rattler in the grass
Amarillo dies for el sol
Violeta flows out of the sunset
Naranja leaps in el incendio

GET READY

I am the wind
I am the rain
I am the lightning
I am the thunder
I am the storm itself
I am the volcano's smoke and fire
I am the earth's beating heart
I am the ocean tide
I am billions of people together pushing in one direction
I am the change that's coming
I am a new day
I am the unfolding flowers
No one can stop me
Ready or not
   Here I come!

*Yo nací en 1980 en Yákima
y soy criada en México. Me
gusta arreglar flores en agua
fría. Me gustaría arreglar
todas las flores que hay.*

*In 1980 I was born in
Yakima and raised in
Mexico. Now I live in
Seattle. I enjoy arranging
flowers in cold water. I'd
like to arrange all the
flowers there are.*

VERONICA CASTAÑEDA

AGUZADERA

La punta mojada es, para mí, que es una punta mojada
y es en el verano y oí
que hacen el cuchillo
con la piedra
y mojada
lo hacen el cuchillo
filoso

WHETSTONE

The wet point is, for me, what is a wet point
and it is summer and I heard
they stroke the knife
over stone
and wet
they make the knife
sharp.

YO SOY Y YO QUISIERA SER

Yo soy una mariposa de muchos colores

yo no quisiera ser un muerto
o una bruja
o una televisión grande

Yo pienso que soy y quisiera ser otra cosa
una silla, una puerta o un pizarrón
o quisiera ser un gusanito que no pica

Y yo no quiero ser como la basura
u otra niña
o una grabadora que toque todos los días.

Quisiera trabajar en El Centro de la Raza
quisiera ser una luz prendida toda la noche y el día
o ser una pintura que es apreciada sumamente

O una blusa de modelo
unos zapatos altos
que se lujan mucho

o me gustaría trabajar en un restaurante que está bien grande
o al elevador de Seattle que rasca los cielos
o con pájaros tropicales que están nostálgicos

Y me gustaría ser una muchacha bonita
que se luje mucho en su belleza
y siempre está a la merced tierna de mis propias travesuras.

I AM AND I WOULD LIKE TO BE

I am a rainbow colored butterfly

I wouldn't want to be someone dead
a bruja
or a huge television set

I think that I am and would like to be something else
a chair, a door or a chalkboard
or be a little caterpillar that doesn't bite

but I don't want to be like throw-away trash
nor another child
nor a record player that plays nonstop day in day out

I would like to work at El Centro de la Raza
or be a light shining noon and night
or I would like to be a painting highly valued

Or a model's blouse
a pair of pricey high heel pumps
that shine

Or I would like to work in a huge five-star restaurant
or Seattle's Space Needle that pokes the sky
or with tropical birds very homesick.

And I would hope to be a lovely young woman
who luxuriates in her beauty
and is always at the tender mercy of her own pranks and wit.

Nacio en Toluca, México en 1974. El vive en Ciudad México. Está estudiando abagacía. El viene a Seattle de vecita y trabaja como voluntario en El Centro de la Raza.

Born in Toluca, Mexico in 1974, Sergio Chagoya lives in Mexico City and is studying to become a lawyer. He visits Seattle and volunteers at El Centro de la Raza.

SERGIO CHAGOYA

XINANTECATL

Xinantecatl montaña majestuosa
rodeada por inmensos árboles,
símbolo de la magnificencia de la naturaleza.
En tu seno admiro dos lagunas
que son como tus ojos
ojos que reflejan el sentido
de tu alma indígena, porque
son como ellos rígido, pero
con una belleza profunda
y mística.

XINANTECATL

Majestic mountain surrounded by vast trees
symbol of nature's magnificance.
Inside your cone I admire two lagoons
much like eyes,
eyes that reflect the essence of your indigenous soul.
They are deeply still but have
a profound and mystic beauty.

Chantay Contreras was born in 1980 and lives in Los Angeles, California. She likes to swim and ride horses. She goes to El Centro de la Raza when she visits Seattle.

CHANTAY CONTRERAS

I AM

I am a locked door
I am a pineapple
I am a tiger
I am an earring
I am a t-shirt
I am a turtle
I am a book
I am a chair
I am a table
I am Mexican and American.

Ernesto Cardenal

VISION FROM THE BLUE WINDOW

From the round window, everything is blue,
the earth bluish, blue-green, blue
                                        (sky blue)

              everything is blue
blue lakes and lagoons
                  blue volcanoes
the further away the land, the bluer it is
     blue islands in a blue lake.
This is the face of the liberated land.
And where all the people fought, I think:
                                        for love!
To live without exploitation's
                            hatred.
To love each other in a lovely land
very lovely, not only for the land
              but for its people
above all for its people.
That's why God rendered it so lovely
for its society.
And in all those blue places they fought, they suffered
              for a society of love
                        here in this land.
A bit of blue has greater intensity…
And it seemed to me I was seeing the places of all the battles,
and all the deaths,
that, behind this glass, small, round,
                              blue
              I was seeing all the shades of blue.

Translated by Marc Zimmerman

Pinanganak sa Manila noong Marso 9, 1981. Siya ay lumipat dito sa Seattle noong Hulyo 1991. Ang una niyang alam no salita ay Tagalog na salita sa Luzon, Pilipinas. Ito ay isa sa mga karamihang salita na galing sa bokabolaryong Kastilá.

Born in Manila on March 9, 1981, Jonathan Diaz moved to Seattle in July 1991. His first language is Tagalog indigenous to Luzon in the Phillipines which is one of many languages that utilizes Spanish.

JONATHAN DIAZ

PAGSASALIN

Sa isang lumang larawan
   nakita ko ang isang pamilya
      na may isang sanggol
         na tumatawa sa kusina

Sa isang lumang kuwadra
   nakita ko ang isang kabayo
      at isang lumang kalabasa
Ang bahay ay
   malapit sa isang sementeryo
      ano ang nangyayari
         ang tanong ng isang quin-oo.

TRANSLATING

In an old foto
  I saw a familia
    with a baby
      cooing in the cocina

I saw a caballo in the barn
  and an old calabaza

The casa sits
  near a cementerio
   and a caballero
    asks que pasa.

Ang kanyang aguela ay si Bermosa Dumlao. Si Nerissa ay pinanganak noong Enero 22, 1982 sa Maynila.

Nerissa Diaz's grandmother is Bermosa Dumlao. Nerissa was born on January 22, 1982 in Manilla, Phillipines.

NERISSA DIAZ

ANG AKING LOLA

Ang lola ko ay kamukha ng isang galit na buwan.
Dahil kung ang bahay ay napakarumi itoy kanyang nililinis.
Kung siyay pumunta sa palengke
At bumalik siya na marumi ang bahay
Ito ay dahil marami kami sa pamilya.
Pitong matatanda at siyam na bata.
Kaya ang lola ko ay kamukha ng galit na buwan.

MY GRANDMOTHER

My grandmother looks like an angry moon
because if the house is very dirty
she cleans it.
If she goes to market
and comes back to a dirty house again
it's because we have lots of family—
seven adults and nine children.
That's why
my grandmother looks like an angry moon.

HARAP HARAPAN

Sa kauna-unahan kong pagpunta
   sa inuman upang uminum
     may tumulak sa akin sa likod at ang tubig ay umakyat.
Hanggang sa aking ilong.

Umiyak ako ng bahagya at tumakbo ako sa opisina
     upang isumbong sa punong-guro ngunit wala siya doon.
      Nakita ko ang isang guro
at sinabi niya sa bata na huwag akong itulak muli.

Nang oras ng pananghali-an sa lugar ng aming pinglaru-an
    itinulak ako ng bata. Natakot ako.
     Tiningnan ko siya sa mukha
at sinabi ko na akoy si Nerissa
        Huwag mo akong itulak
      Ibig kong maging kaibigan mo.

FACE TO FACE

The very first time I went to the fountain
    to get a drink
        somebody pushed me in the back.
The water went up my nose.

I cried a little bit and ran to the office
    to tell the principal who was not there.
        I found a teacher
and he told the boy not to push me again.

Lunch recess the boy pushed me in the play court.
    It scared me.
        I looked at him in the face
and I said my name is Nerissa
            Don't push me
                I want to be your friend.

His mother is from Chicago and his father is from Phoenix, he was born in Salem, Oregon on August 29, 1979.

ELLIS FOSTER

IF I COULD

If I could I would be twenty-one
If I could I would change the way some people act
If I could I would be rich and famous

If I could I would wish homes for them
people who are out busted on the streets

If I could I would change the world
If I could I would change me first
If I could!

MY PINE TREE

I had a pine tree in my backyard.
When I was feeling down
I'd sit by that tree
and it would make me feel better.
Sometimes I would try to hug it
but it was too big.

Once when I was sitting by my pine tree
I heard my mom turn up the music
so she couldn't hear my baby sister cry.
I ran away to my friend's house
to get away.

When I returned home my mom asked
where have you been all this time
said by the way your dad cut down your tree
because we needed it for firewood.

I ran to my room and shut the door
thinking oh no mom
how could you do this to me.
I didn't come out until the next day.

THE BIG DANCE

I felt anxious to get to the dance
so did my sister.

When we got to the dance
some guys drove up in a black car.

It was shiny with chrome wheels
looking like a black bull in the night
just escaped from the corral.

Suddenly we heard a shot.
I was scared
because it could have hit us.

HUMSY KOY MUNG

On the first day of school
I was playing kickball
when this boy yelled "You're out!"
I hollered "No!"
For a couple of minutes
he hooted "Out! Out! Out!"
We argued until I yelled
"Yo! Boy, shut up or be stupid!"

We stopped.
When we got on the bus
he came to me and said
"Humsy koy mung"
I want to be your friend in Lao.

That's how our friendship started.

Born in Los Angeles on October 31, 1978, he follows his sports heros Walter Payton, Michael Jordan and Ken Griffey, Jr.

EDVENT GRINNELL III

LIKE THEM

I want to be like Walter Payton, Michael Jordan
or Ken Griffey, Jr.
because they are my idols.

I've always wanted to be like them.

Everytime I see Michael Jordan play
I want him to slam dunk
and when I see Payton run with the ball
I think he's going to score.
He runs so fast.
When Griffey is up to bat
I say I hope he hits a home run.

I like them for being them.

DRUGS

Drugs are an icky wicky thing
that people use.

They think that it is fun.
Drugs will get you high
but you can die.

If you sell drugs
you are killing someone and yourself.

Drug dealers drug people
for money,

they don't care about people
all they care about is money.

*Born April 30, 1981 in Sa-
lem, Oregon, she partici-
pates in jump roping com-
petitions with her team the
Popcorns. She wants to be
a physician to treat children
and the homeless.*

TIERRA GREIG

WHEN I FELT LIKE
RUNNING AWAY

Once My mom yelled at me
cuz I hit my little brother.
She thought I talked back.
I started to cry.
When my grandmother called
I asked her if I could live with her.
She said no.
I started crying again
and went to my room.
I started to pack my stuff.
I stopped to write to my friend
who lived down the street.

Dear LeFawné
Can I come live with you?
I'll feed your hamsters.
Love, Tierra.

I called LeFawné
and her mom said no
cuz they didn't have enough room.
I put the letter in my jewel box
so no one could find it.

Instead of running away
I hid in my closet.

I thought my mom
would get in a better mood
but she was crying
and in the worst mood
she'd ever been in before.
Then I heard my mom
say time for dinner
and I smelled the pizza.
I left the closet
to give my mother a big hug
and to tell her sorry.
She said don't do that again
and I never did.

Born March 24, 1983 in Seattle, she wants to become a veterinarian. She gets hands-on computer experience learning about the travel agency business from her mother Rosamaría Rosales. Her parents are from Mexico.

JANET GUZMAN

GUM

I like purple gum because it's purple.
I like to chew gum that's hot.
I ate hot gum this afternoon
but I can't eat it everyday or I'll get sick.

If I blow bubbles
they will pop and stick in my hair.
When I try to take the gum out
I pull out my hair.

OLIVIA SILVA'S RÍO TULE

I see the blue and green sky
I see the green river
I see green and brown leaf trees.
I see swans, parrots and rare birds.
I see red violet blossoms.
I want to jump into the river and swim.

A MÍ NO ME GUSTA / A MÍ ME GUSTA

A mí no me gusta:
1. Cuando Osita me muerde
2. Los vestidos
3. Las zanahorias y los frijoles
4. Muelas porque me duelen
5. Salsa picante

A mí me gusta:
1. Osita
2. Pastel con helado
3. Mi cumpleaños
4. Los shorts en marzo
5. Los mangos ricos
6. Zoë, mi maestra de poesía
7. La nieve porque its yummy to eat
8. Mi pelota de un tamaño de una cereza.

Mirna Martínez

ARS POETICA

I want blue to color all my years. (After all they
are too few and
even a thousand years later their sum
will still be too few.)
I want blues to stain my hands.
I want blues to flood my eyes.
I want blues to color my tongue.
I want blues blues blues: death
is not important to me
if blue is for this epoch.
I want all my texts to be blue
and this is not anachronistic to history
it's just that for me
blue is…(i don't know how to say it)
blue is…
      one more tone of red.

Translation by Zoë Anglesey

I was born in Seattle, Washington at Swedish Medical Center on August 3, 1979. I like sports including football, swimming, baseball and basketball too. My best friends are Sandra and Rashaad.

SHAY HATTON

I JUST DO WHAT MATTERS TO ME

Weed's not nothin to me
until the dealer tries to sell it to me
and my friends.

I would say don't you know
what you are doing to brothers and sisters.

Drugs aren't nothin to me.

If someone shoots me in the head
it still would add up to nothin.

In that case, I'm gone.

Kenia Lewis grew up in Ensenada located in Baja, Mexico. She now lives in Seattle.

KENIA LEWIS

LA PALABRA

es poderosa
e importante para nuestro pueblo.
Pienso que puede ayudarnos
pero también dañarnos.
Puede hacernos cambiar de sentimientos.
Por ejemplo si estoy triste
pero alguien me dice
no te preocupes
te quiero
me sentiré feliz.
Sí estoy feliz y alguien me dice
una palabra desagradable
me sentiré triste.
Es inolvidable.

Y debemos de tener cuidado
y pensar acerca de esa palabra
antes de que salga de nosotros.

THE WORD

is powerful
and important to our community.
I think it can help us
but it can hurt us too.
A word can make us change our feelings.
For example, if I'm sad
and someone says to me
don't worry
I love you
it will make me feel happy.
If I am happy and someone says
an unfriendly word to me
I will feel sad.
It's unforgettable.
We should be careful and think
about the meaning each word has
before we say it.

Born in Groton, Connecticut in 1977; she has lived in Europe and moved from Bremerton to Orlando, Florida. Her father worked for the Navy. Her sister, Melissa Lopez, works at El Centro de la Raza.

MONICA LOPEZ

WAITING

She's out on the corner waiting for someone
who will come and take her away.
She ran away when she was twelve
hoping life would be better
but she was wrong.
She lives on the streets
and hasn't eaten right for weeks.
She's waiting on this corner
waiting for someone.

DRUGS USE AND ABUSE YOUR MIND

Drugs—what good do they do?
They use and abuse your mind
have you think it's just a spell
and make your life a living hell!

People come and people go
because they can't keep up with the flow
then they end up dead
with a bullet through their head
because someone on drugs
can't think up something to do
instead of drugs.

He writes: One of the best days of my life was when I met Mayor Norm Rice; one of the worst was when I broke some dishes. He was born in San Diego on November 30, 1982.

FRED MAINOR

THE CHINA STAR

In the boys locker room
a kid yelled do you want me to throw
this China Star at you.

I said no
and to myself
that sure is a stupid question.

In his hand, he held the China Star
a corolla of blades
bright, shiny and razor sharp.

I walked through the door
as quickly as I could
and jumped into the pool.

I swam and swam laps
hoping to forget the danger
that the China Star threatened.

LOS DULCES

Los dulces taste delicious
but they rot your teeth

In Mexico on the Day of the Dead
kids eat candy skeletons in a casket

Los dulces of sugar are skulls
with the names of Luisa
Jaime, Federico and Georgina.

Los dulces called the dead heads
wear frosting sombreros.

Los dulces go ten for a peso
weighing less than a handful.

KID'S STUFF

If you're a kid you're lucky.
If you're a grownup you're not
because kids do more things like
chewing gum, jumping rope,
gymnastics and playing games.

Parents always say they wish
they were kids again when they talk
about things they did in the 1960s.
They say those were the good old days.

Whenever anybody asks what you're doing
just say kid stuff!

*Born August 24, 1981, she
did the splits at age four.
Active in gymnastics and
jump roping, she is a team
member of The Popcorns.*

LEFAWNÉ MAINOR

JUSTICIA

Justicia opens up to goodness and fairness
Justicia works for la paz
Justicia means Bonita María Gustón, my friend
Justicia talks linda
Justicia sometimes está durmiendo
Justicia needs to be fought for
Justicia demands that some people
                             say adios to their lives.

PEOPLE

People like me care about people
People like me can do things if they want to
People like me like to jump rope
People like this like themselves
because people love you.

Born in Seattle, July 7, 1982, he started school at El Centro de la Raza's José Martí Child Development Center and has been a part of the youth program ever since.

ARMANDO MARTINEZ

INSULTS

I hate it when people call
each other names.

They both get hurt
the one who suffers the insult
and the one who throws the word.

The ugliness of the world increases.

THE NAVAJO HUNTER

rides a blue horse
throws his spear
at the buffalo.
His knife flies off his back.
He yanks the horse's reins.

His friends attack more buffalo.

This night
they will enjoy a feast.

TO THE DANCE THEATER OF HARLEM

Firebird
are you going to be as mean
as you are red?
Oh, I saw you give a feather to the prince.
I got it, you must be nice.
You are destroying evil spirits.
I saw your feathers candy apple red
and I said
so pretty.

BLACK

I want black to stay with me.
I have a black watch and black shoes
black pants
black hair
black eyes.
Oh! I got everything black.
I want to go to Alaska and fish in black water.
I like M.C. Hammer.
He's black and he's a black singer.
I like black olives on my pizza.
I want a black Ferrari
because I like to move fast.
I look at girls with black hair.

CHINANGO

Chinango! I can't go to sleep
Chinango! I eat your burritos
Chinango! Don't growl at me
Chinango! I'm going to pull your ears

Chinango! Your donkeys stink!
Chinango! Let me dance with your mamasita
Chinango! I put mangos on your altar
Chinango! Are you a place of safety?

Chinango! I hope killers don't follow your young
Chinango! To rocks, cactus and flowers
Chinango! I can't wait to visit your hideaways.

THE TRUTH

During the day I get in trouble!   Psych!
I run in front of cars.   Psych!
I play baseball professionally.   Psych!
I walk through walls and jump out the window.   Psych!

Her family is from Toppenish, Washington; her mother has twelve brothers and sisters. Born on December 24, 1979, she is Mexican. She likes sports and horse back riding.

SANDRA MARTINEZ

GARIBALDI PARK
IN MEXICO CITY

Blue corazón danced on the stones
cuando la mujer was tocando la música.

On the street los carros laughed
and tonight is the final night.

THURSDAY ON THE BUS

We caught the number seven
across the street from Chuck's.

At the bus stop in front of Franklin
two groups of guys got on
and sat in the front.

One started to slap another guy
on the back of his head.
The black guys got off
and ran for McDonalds.
The white guys followed.

From the bus window we saw the black guys stop
turn around and pull up their shirts.
All of them had guns
tucked in at the belt.

The white guys ran across the street
yelling names.
When the bus turned
we couldn't see anymore.

WEARING RED

Juan and Mo
wore red shirts.
Chris had on red shorts.

Chris matched.
Juan's shoes got to go
but otherwise Mo looked okay.

I took the fire extinguisher
and just had to spray.

Born January 18, 1983, in Dallas, Texas, she has also lived in Bremerton, Washington. Ashley's mother, Helen McDonald, volunteers at El Centro de la Raza.

ASHLEY MCDONALD

KICKING

Me and my homegirl be
kicking at the sports court
lickin some flave.

We be flirting with the fellows
so we can party
kick back n rap dance.

IT MAKES US DIE

I don't like pollution
it makes the rivers cry

I don't like pollution
the trees fall down and die

I don't like pollution
the smoke in the air blocks the sky

I don't like pollution
it tells the whole wide world goodbye.

THE MAGIC SHOP

When we went to the magic shop
we saw candy that could make you sorry
and gum if you chewed it
would make your mouth turn blue
and a tea bag that smelled bad enough
to make you gag the minute it hit some water.
Most of all I liked the magic bean.
When you soaked it
it swelled into a panda.

Ernesto Cardenal

THE PARROTS

My friend Michel is the military leader in Somoto,
       there near the border with Honduras,
and he told me that he discovered a contraband shipment of parrots
set for export to the U.S.
       so that there they would learn to speak English.
There were 186 parrots, and 47 had already died in their cages.
And he sent them back where they'd come from,
and when the truck reached a place
         they call The Plains
near the mountain homes of these parrots
       (the mountains looked huge
             rising from these plains)
the parrots began to stir and beat their wings
       and jam themselves against their cage walls.
And when the cages were opened
they all flew out like arrows in the same direction
             toward their mountains.
This is the same thing, I think, that the Revolution did to us:
it took us out of the cages
       in which they'd carried us off to speak English.
It brought us back the homeland from which they'd uprooted us.

The soldiers green like parrots
         gave the parrots their green mountains.
   But there were 47 who died.

Translated by Marc Zimmerman

Nacida en León, México, febrero 3, 1983, Susana Mendoza le gusta leer y discutir en lenguajes diferentes.

Born in Leon, Mexico on February 3, 1983, Susana Mendoza likes to read and speak different languages.

SUSANA MENDOZA

YO IMAGINO

Yo soy una mujer muy adulta
con muchas bonitas flores en mis manos.

Yo siento que me esta dibujando
de una artista con lapiz brillante.

Yo veo los colores de mi vestido
floreciendo en el papel blanco.

La artista quiere de titulo a la pintura.
Yo le oigo diciendo mi nombre.

I IMAGINE

I am a woman all grown up
with beautiful flowers in my hands.

I feel like I am being drawn
by an artist holding a shiny pencil.

I see the colors of my dress
blossom on the white paper.

The artist wants to title the painting.
I hear him saying my name.

Born in Kennewick in eastern Washington on May 18, 1981, she moved from Pasco to Seattle at age six. She has been attending El Centro de la Raza since going to the José Martí Child Development Center. She wants to be a lawyer.

ELISA MIRANDA

YOURSELF INSIDE

You look inside a lake
you see a mirror
and you see yourself inside.
You cry
over your crying face.

BE CAREFUL WITH YOUR LIFE

You come from a town that is loving
then you move to the city
and you meet some friends who do drugs.

But they're cool where ever you go
so you join them.
Then you go on your first strike.

When the cops come you are lost
you don't feel smart any more.

You go to jail
and you feel stupid.

When you get out
you go back to your friends
and you tell them I quit.

The next day you are killed.

WHEN I DIE

When I die my dry black hair
will not fly like a flock in the wind

When I die my eyes won't see
the ones I love

When I die I won't hear as before
the birds in their voices

When I die I will remember the aroma
of the sea

When I die my tongue won't taste
the strawberry's flesh, juice or seed

When I die place my hands
on my heart

When I die my feet will take me to
both sides of the Rio Grande.

SECRETS

I whisper to my friend
about something I can't tell you
really something quite natural.

Well, here's a little hint
it's something that only girls like.

Something very personal
it's important that we talk and talk about it.

When our teacher looks up
she sees us with our hands to our mouths
full of secrets.

That gives us no choice
but to finish our conversation
at recess.

NATURE'S PATH

Outside playing you see a rose and a cornflower
twisted together.
You go to pick them
and look around and you're lost.
Below the flowers there is a crystal.
You rub the dirt off and put it in your pocket.
Then you go to a place where there's a bunch of bamboo.
You get one of the leaves
and you put it in another pocket.
You look up in the sky and you hardly see the sun.
You keep on following the trail
until you see a big waterfall
and you drink from it.
Then you go to a sandy part of the river's edge.
You find a crab shell
next to big letters that spell R A M O N!
And then you find the path.

THINKING ABOUT ERNESTO CARDENAL'S "PARROTS"

You and me think we'll be free forever.
One day men come to the forest to hunt for us
and we're put in little cages.
We feel like we've been trapped forever.
We think we'll never see a tree again.

We are packed on a plane
and some of us suffocate to death.

A few of us make it to the same store.
People buy us and put us in a tiny cage.
They are mean and don't treat us right
they only give us food and water.

At last their baby girl grows up.
She takes us back on a plane
where we can finally live
in our natural home.

CÁLLATE!

Boeing jet plane overhead
I can't say a word to my friend she can hear. Cállate!

Honking honky horns
do you have to honk in a hospital zone? Cállate!

Mr. President, when you say the poor don't get jobs
cuz they're too lazy to work, I scream...Cállate!

Devon, don't yell in my ear
my eardrums will pop. Cállate!

Mom, will you let me sleep
just a little bit longer? Cállate!

Miss Hedeen, when I'm in the middle of my favorite book
you say put everything away; that's when I want to say, Cállate!

Lacey, just because you're bigger
doesn't mean you can tease me. Cállate!

When I want to hear a million crickets
over the hills in homey's Pasco, I whisper

Diego, Armando, Sandra, Paul and Tony...Cállate!

MY QUESTION
AT TEN YEARS OLD

I wonder everyday what I'm going to be—

The target of knifing blades
or the thunder in the barrel of the gun
that kills?

Born December 13, 1972 in Moses Lake. In Seattle, he graduated from Nathan Hale High School, the first to do so in his family. In the eleventh grade he played husband and father in the play Sí, Se Puede performed at El Centro de la Raza.

JAKE MIRANDA

METAPHOR

Life in this world passes for a banana.
You peel it.
You see one end smooth
and edible
or the other end bruised.

I WOULDN'T MIND BEING A KID

I would like to be a seabird
or a river that flows through rain

a flower bright with sunshine
or something that glows at night
be something delicate as a petal
or a smile on an open face.

I wouldn't mind being a kid
for the curiosity and fun they have
or the love they give and take.

MACKED

She looks pretty swas
when she dances down the street

He almost got the girl
in the sack

He almost macked that girl
but in a quick second she thought twice

and burnt him to a crisp.

ODE TO SHIRTS

I like short-sleeved shirts
cotton and kitten soft.

They soak in all the sweat
from the mind-busting work I do.

I wear long-sleeved
good-looking shirts when I go dancing
loose shirts
that let me do a lot of loose things.

She lived in Mt. Vernon, Washington, California and a year on Orcus Island. She was born on January 1, 1984 and likes to dance, roller and ice skate.

LILY OSTLE

FIRST POEM

When a man kills
a man dies
inside.

I was born deep in the heart of Texas, in San Antonio, on the 30th day of October in 1971. All of my relatives were born in Texas except, on a vacation trip to Mexico, my great grandparents gave birth to Maria de la luz Piña, the sweet mother of my father and my very much missed aunts and uncles. I always wish for equal rights for women, men, people of all heritages, for animals and especially for the abused, but beautiful earth. I don't get angry easy, but like my scalp, I'm sensitive.

JAVIER PIÑA

LIKE THE NORTH STAR

Squinting in the brightness, making me walk
only by sound, feel and smell

I heard the sound of an old muffler
and untuned engine.
I caught the odor of cheap gas
and garbage rotting
a permanent stigma of the street.

After a long day in school
I saw the big blue blur
that was our five minute ride home.
I called it the fume-a-gator
and my mom—her "baby blue"
but was nothin more than a heater on wheels.

Tickled by beads of sweat
running down my back
I lifted the handle to the door
that wanted to stay stuck.
I heard my mother's welcoming voice say
"Hey Dude."
Despite the feverish temperature
this always brought a smile to my face.

Here I am
a sixteen year old kid
with a childish grin on my face
as I kiss the sweat off my mother's cheek.

If I had a really bad day
one that would almost compare to Black Thursday
as soon as I was with my mom
the whole world seemed to be Disneyland.

She sat there in her beloved poor excuse of a car
with no sign of age
only the times
with flaming hair
that fit the picture of the day.

What made it interesting
were the bronze red streaks
growing from the black roots.
She was like no other parent
more original than the Mona Lisa
just as beautiful as the Pieta.
In a crowd
she stood out like the north star.

I remember sitting on the warm hood
of the fume-a-gator
after a long tiresome day at work
talking with my friend, my mother,

about our problems
which we wished would burn away
as did the cigarettes we sucked.

Sometimes we just stared at the smoke
that diluted in the air
just like each night of comforting talk.

The birds would wake me for school.
Mom would chime in "Get up Dude."
She would giggle as I stumbled into the bathroom
like some poor drunk.
In the shower I saw from the window
the familiar sun rising from the edge of the earth
to melt us away.

BILINGUAL IN A CARDBOARD BOX

Soy Mexicano
I'm an American

Puedo cantar canciones del corazón
I am mute

Puedo ver los colores de la puesta del sol
I am blind

Puedo escuchar las voces de los pajaritos cantando
I am deaf

Soy indígena bailando al cielo que llora
I'm forever seated in a chair with wheels

Todos me respetan
I'm labeled by pointing fingers

Tengo mucho dinero
I live in a cardboard box

Estoy riéndome con el mundo alegre
I am sad

Salgo con mis amigos
I am alone

Estoy soñando
and I don't want to wake up!

CHARLIE'S GHOST

Sitting on the curb staring at your barely covered feet
the chill seeps through your pants insulated with dirt.
Not meant to match, your clothes keep you warm
in the summer and leave you in the winter quaking cold.
You sit there slumped trying to absorb your own body heat.

Too embarassed to look up to see the eyes
of children or their parents turning heads
as they sit in warm upholstered cars
you can't help think: where did I go wrong.
The Charlie rips away your happy memories
and all you see are flashbacks.

Everyone at home for whom you gave your life ignores you.
The only thing you have left is a rusty insignia
which at one time reflected your glow.
You sit there with a broken back and heart
with no will to beat.

SPANISH-SPEAKING

When I was un chavalón
I remember hearing the word minority.
I always thought it meant los chicos
because minor is small and major is big.
I never knew it was el nombre of our people
who are other than los gabachos.
Are there not enough of us in this mundo
to measure up to the gabacho?

Like them of different colores
we pump sangre out of our corazón
to absorb la vida.
Me pongo malo when I
hear our people called minorities
being labeled without our history
that makes them look at us as basura.

We are victims of injustice
and the way things are going
it's hard to see la luz.

If Sam is our tio and we are all iguales
then there are no more negroes, bolillos
chinos or mojados
there is only one majority
the majority of the human raza

and we are in las Américas.
In the U.S.A.
we are the fastest growing.

Born on September 14, 1977 in Seattle, she lives with each of her divorced parents a half week. She participates in activities and volunteers at El Centro de la Raza.

KRISTY POOLE

AN ODE TO THE PARTS OF ME

I praise my hands
  so very strong
    cuz they'll never hurt
      nor do any wrong.

I praise my eye
  so very thankfully.
    With them I'm always careful
      they help me see.

I praise my feet.
  More than you know
    they always take me
      where I want to go.

I praise my body
  that holds the treasure
    that is me
      in this world of now
        but not forever.

*Born September 23 1982,
he lives close to El Centro
de la Raza on Beacon Hill.
He likes basketball and rap.*

DEVON REED

I HATE FOR KIDS TO DIE

Some kids are dying when
they are only nine or ten.

Every time I hear reporters say
kids have died from gunshot wounds
I turn the channel.

I don't like to hear about
kids my age who have died.

Monica Mansour

CENOTE

cenote
tranquil water
roots dart from the river bed
to reach the blue of sky
and tangle in branches of the closest tree
your mouths breathe in the planetary air
twin rays fire from the cobalt
toward the dark shade of your solemn stones
and they stay wedded to water

I scan your serene impenetrable face
the coolness you do not render to the sun
and I also bear in mind your veins in the earth
where the sufferings of history course
under our heavy footsteps

I disturb your composure
then the sun ignites me

Translation by Zoë Anglesey

Yo nací en Ameca, Jalisco el treinta de enero del 1983. Viví en un pueblo llamado Hacienda del Cabezón. Yo tenía una perrita que se llamaba Geíza. También tenía chivitos. Yo era feliz en mi casa, muy feliz.

I was born in Ameca, Jalisco on January 30th of 1983. I lived in a town named Hacienda del Cabezón. I had a puppy named Geíza. I also had kid goats. I was happy at home, very happy.

JUAN FRANCISCO RUÍZ GARCÍA

AYUTLA

En Ayutla yo me subí
a un burro
y me tumbé
en una piedra resbalosa
y me aplasté el pie
y no me dolió.

AYUTLA

In Ayutla I climbed on
a burro.
We stumbled
over a slippery rock
and I fell under the burro's foot
but it didn't hurt me.

MIS TIEMPOS LIBRES

Una vez yo me subí al burro
mas bonito en Ayutla.

Me llevaba hasta el río
de mi pueblo
Chorros de Tala.

Me divertía con mis amiguitos.
Yo recuerdo nadando
en mis tiempos libres.

IN MY CAREFREE DAYS

Once I climbed onto the most beautiful burro
in Ayutla.

It took me to the river
Chorros de Tala
near my town.

I had fun with my childhood friends.
I remember swimming
in my carefree days.

CHORROS DE TALA

El río Chorros de Tala
caen los chorros de arriba
de una montañita
y por debajo te bañas a gusto.

CHORROS DE TALA

The Chorros de Tala river
drops its waterfalls high
off the top of a little mountain.
Underneath you swim
so happy.

Nací en Ayutla, Jalisco el 1 de mayo de 1980. En mi casa tenía tres perros, gatos, chivos, puercos, borrego, gallinas, y patos. Aquí en Seattle estoy muy bien y se me hace bonito.

I was born on May 1, 1980 in Ayutla, Jalisco. At home I had three dogs, cats, goats, pigs, a lamb, chickens and ducks. Here in Seattle I'm doing fine and all is going beautifully.

GABRIELA RUÍZ SANTANA

LA RAZA

Aquí sobre la tierra
hay varios colores
y colores de piel.

Por ejemplo
blancos, negros, morenos
de varios colores.

Yo existo dentro
de la distinción
entre nosotros

Y eso no es bueno porque se supone
que Diós nos hizo a todos
y no se deben de burlar
de nuestros colores.

LA RAZA

Here on earth
there are various colors
and colors of skin.

For example
whites, blacks, browns
of so many tones.

I exist within
prejudices
among us

That's not right because it's
assumed that God made us all
and no one should ridicule
our many colors.

AYUTLA ES BONITA

Ayutla es bonita
porque allí no usan drogas
pero tampoco toman tanto

No pasan accidentes
ni se ponen tomadores en las esquinas
solos en las cantinas.

Para estar saludable
es no seguir las drogas
ni el vino
ni las otras cosas vergonzosas.

AYUTLA IS BEAUTIFUL

Ayutla is beautiful
because there they don't use drugs
however they drink too much.

Accidents don't happen
and boozers don't hang out on corners
only inside the bars.

So as to stay healthy
don't get hooked on drugs
nor wine
or other disgraceful things.

EN EL BOSQUE

Hay patines rojos volando en el cielo
y las amapolas plantadas en la tierra.

Ese bosque me gusta
porque hay naturaleza

Y flores lindas y pájaros
que cantan
y alegran el bosque.

IN THE FOREST

There are red gooseducks flying in the sky
and hibiscus planted in the ground

I adore that forest
because of nature

The gorgeous flowers and birds
that sing
and make the forest happy.

Born July 13, 1977 in Bogotá, Colombia, he moved to Miami in 1978 and then to Seattle.

JUAN CARLOS SANCHEZ

THINK ABOUT IT

Everyday I'm walking in the street.
I turn my head and see kids with prostitutes
who walk around unashamed
ruining our youth.

It's a pity that people choose that way to live.
Maybe someday they will know what they are doing
take a chill pill
and think about it.

Born May 3, 1977 in Seattle, she is Swedish, German, Norwegian and Italian by way of her mother. From her dad's family she is French, Native and African American. She plans to become a pediatrician.

CHARNITA ANN SAWYER

MODERN LIFE

Me and my homeys be chillin outside in the parking lot
thinking why we're not with our families.
Mom is trippin and dad is flippin over some stupid reasoning.
Brothers and sisters are fighting over dope.

Grandma and grandpa are takin care of their grandchildren
when they know who should be carin for them.
You know how it used to be: after work mom at home
in the kitchen and dad on his job.

No it ain't like that no more.
Now it's mom snortin crack and dad pushin rock.
Pushers and pimps run the streets.
Hookers wonder when they'll be beat.

Eloy Tenorio was born in Santa Fe, New Mexico on April 30, 1980.

ELOY TENORIO

WHAT A HAIRCUT CAN DO UNTO YOU

I went to a barber shop
happy
then I opened the big door.
I waited for two minutes watching television.

I stood up and walked to a chair.
As I sat on the cold seat
the barber pulled out a large clean cloth
that felt like a sheet of ice.
The barber snipped as fast as Edward scissor hands
with a big pair of shears.
My hair fell down in slow motion.
I didn't know my bangs were that long.

The next day at school
a kid walked up to me and asked
what happened to your hair.

I thought in my mind
that was only one person
there are others
who will appreciate my haircut.

A group of kids came up to me
with their mouths wide open in laughter
while my eyes filled
red in anger.

A week later no one noticed my hair at all.

Born in Santa Fe, New Mexico on April 5, 1984, Juan enjoys turning out for sports.

JUAN TENORIO

LOOKING AT A DRAWING
BY GABRIEL MORALES

A skull
two fighters dance around it.

Death laughs at them and knows
they will go to it soon.

We should stop feeding death
and feed the hungry.

YO! EL LOBO!

I met a señora and her señor walking down the street
with un lobo blanco.
I said "Yo! Hola! I'm your brother."

The señora and her señor were from Honolulu
so they said "Aloha!"

I said "Hasta luego."

I forgot how they said it
but the señora and her señor
waved "Bye" in Hawaiian.

ON THE SUBJECT OF...

I'm glad that Nintendo bought the Mariners
so when it's baseball season
my sister, my brother, my dad and I
can watch the games.

My brother plays baseball
for the Kent Park team.
I play during basketball season
my team is the Blazers.

My birthday is on April 5th.
I'm going to have everyone on my team over
for a party, even my parents
and all the good kids in my class.

Everyday I like to read very big
and fat books
for example:

Dr. Seuss
Crash
Chicka Chicka Boom Boom
Merry Melodies and Tiny Tune Adventures
Monkey monkey Tricks
The Three Little Bears
Polar bears.

I admire panda bears
the way they look white and black.

Crash
Chicky chicky chick chick
Ding Dong Ding Dong.

PORQUE DURING VACATION

I wish I could go to Funplex
porque lazer tag, bumpercars and motorcycle marathons
make me feel like I'm living large.

I'm going to Disneyland so I can visit
Miguel, El Ratón.

At Miami Beach
I want to go swimming todos los días.

One of my true wishes would be to expel myself
from school, porque
I hate my principal and her name.

I like cuatro teachers
I have five.

Born October 26, 1979 in Pasadena, California, his heritage from his father's side is Irish, German and Welch, and from his mother's—Irish, English and Mexican. He became involved with the Hope for Youth Program in 1986 when he was seven.

PAUL WILLIAMS

GRANDMOTHER

My mom often tells me what my grandmother was like:
Blonde with hazel eyes, she was fair
and never said goodbye.

I often stare at a photograph of her next to my mom and aunt
laying on the warm silky sand
with the red-hot sun shining on their backs.
I wonder what they were feeling at the time
and if they knew their mother was soon going to die.
The one thing I remember
she used to eat cabbage.
When I asked her for some
she would say
you wouldn't like it.

DRUGS

People who offer themselves to drugs
barely make it out alive.

Doing drugs is like a war
will power versus temptation.

Drugs have spread throughout the nation.
Taking drugs some people deny it
some people regret it
and some people confess to it.

Signs of drug use
spread throughout the body—
first direction toward the mind.

THE BAD SIDE OF TOWN

I was born where smog rules
the pollution center of the world.
People in Los Angeles can't stop polluting.
It's like drugs
you just can't stop.
It's a bad habit
that you can't pull off.

What has the world come to?
It used to be naturally green
with rolling hills
tree-topped mountains and beautiful plains.
Now there's erosion, dust
evaporation
and death.

ODE TO LEVIS

Thank God for levis.
I'd never live without them.
From 50l to 505
Levi jeans just blow my mind.
Blue, black, grey, green
Levi jeans is just livin large.
The difference in each pair of jeans
depends on how you wear them.
They look good cuffed
out-of-style rolled.
Levis are for anyone
who knows how to party.

Roberto Obregón

EQUAL TO A PEBBLE

Words, when exposed to air
grow like calves.
Over the years they mature and increase in value
or they may be stillborn.
Either one.

The word reveals to us
what constitutes the spirit.
It's a very delicate thing.

In the mouth of a liar
it exposes to the bone
a thankless soul.

The word, equal to nuclear power
in good hands can save lives
if not, it amounts to doomsday
in a darkened conscience.

By impact of a word alone
a Hollywood star can fall from grace.
Tyrants fear it
and the guilty prefer not to use it.

Like coins we drop words
into the mind of a child
so that with time
the thinking will be a storehouse of riches.

The word is the most precious of gems
we give to our loved ones
so they believe and confide in us.

If love falls apart it's proof we lie.

A moist word, vital like earth
whispers in the hush of silence
and true it can soothe, be lusty
or instrumental to a plan that urges on a nation.

Sure. People live not by bread alone.
The word also offers sustenance
being what it is:
product of my hands, and yours.
And no such things!

Translated by Zoë Anglesey

GLOSSARY

Agua Pura: Pure water
Alegre: Happy
Amarillo: Yellow
Ayutla: Small town in Mexico
Azul: Blue

Bailando: Dancing
Basura: Garbage, trash
Blanco: White
Bolillos: In Mexico—hard, white bread rolls; whites

Calabaza: Pumpkin, squash or dried gourd
Caballero: Gentleman
Caballo: Horse
Cállate: Be quiet in the command form, silence please
Canción: Song
Cantar: To sing
Casa: House, home
Cereza: Cherry
Chavalón: Young man, hip dude
Chicos: Small, little
Chinango: A town in Mexico
Cielo: Sky, heaven
Cocina: Kitchen
Comer: To eat
Corazón: Heart
Cuando: When

Dinero: Money, wealth
Durmiendo: Sleeping
Duelen: They hurt, ache
Dulces: Sweets, candy

El Incendio: The fire
El Perro: The dog

El Ratón: The rat
El Sol: The sun
Escuchar: To hear or to listen
Es La Verdad: It's the truth
Están: They are
Estoy: I am

Familia: family

Gabachos: Originally meaning from the Pyrenees, French like;
    foreigner, white men

Hola: Hi, hello

Indigéna: Indigenous, native, original peoples

Jalisco: Department (state) in Mexico

Linda: Cute, pretty, attractive
Lobo: Wolf, wild or huge dog
Llorando: Crying
Luz: Light

Maestra: Teacher
Me Duelen: They ache or hurt
Me Gusta: I like
Me Muerde: Bites me
Me Pongo Malo: I get an attitude, I resent
Me Respetan: They respect me
Mira: Look
Mojados: Wet, wetbacks
Muelas: Molars, the vernacular for cavities in molars
Muerde: Bite
Mujer: Woman
Mundo: World, planet

Naranjo: Orange tree; naranja—orange (fruit), orange colored
Nieve: Snow

Nombre: Name

Osita: Diminutive of Osa the feminine form for "little bear."

Pan Dulce: Sweet bread, pastries
Pajaritos: Little birds
Pastel Con Helado: Cake and ice cream
Paz: Peace
Pelota: Ball
Pero: the conjunction, but
Poesía: Poetry
Porque: Because; por qué—why
Puedo Cantar: I can sing
Puesta Del Sol: Sunset

Qué Pasa: What's happening

Rico: Rich, tasty, delicious
Riéndome: I am laughing with or about
Rojo: red

Salgo: I leave
Salsa Picante: Hot sauce
Sangre: Blood
Se Puede: You can, you are able; one can
Soñando: Dreaming
Soy: I am

Tamaño: Size
Tengo: I have
Tierra: Land, ground, earth, country
Tío: Uncle
Todos: All, everyone, total
Tocando: Playing an instrument, playing music

Ver: To see
Verde: green
Vestidos: Dresses

Vida: Life
Violeta: Violet or purple

Zanahorias: Carrots

NOTES

Las Américas: Name for the whole continent, north, central, south and the Caribbean. "America" may have originated from the Mayan-Carib word "Amac Ric"—meaning strong life force, strong wind.

Ernesto Cardenal, former Minister of Culture to the Sandanista government, was born on January 20, 1925 in Grenada, Nicaragua. Recent books include *Los OVNIs de Oro: Poemas Indios/ Golden UFOs: Indian Poems* (Indiana University Press, 1992) and *Cosmic Cantos* (Curbstone Press, 1993), a collection of poems coming at the end of the Twentieth Century which incorporates current ideas concerning the genesis of our universe as defined by quantum theory. He has devoted 1991-1992 to writing poems dedicated to the multiple indigenous cultures that survive in the Americas.

Hermiston Melon for Lunch: Armando Martinez has visited the melon center in Hermiston, Oregon. The Hermiston Melon is a hybrid crossing the watermelon with the honeydew. He recalls doing the serigraph while looking forward to a slice for lunch.

Mirna Martínez, born in El Salvador in 1966, refers to Rubén Darío's poem *Azul* published in 1888 which introduced the modernist movement to the Spanish-speaking countries of the Americas. Darío was responding to the "Blue Movement" of Gautier which had an effect on the symbolist poetry of Paul Verlaine and the Parnassian school of poetry, all of which provides lineage to "Ars Poetica."

"The Navajo Hunter"—This poem was written viewing Quincy Tahoma's painting, *In the Days of the Plentiful*. Quincy Tahoma (Navajo, 1920-1956) lived the life of a shepherd until he started to paint in 1936. *Tamaqua: Native American Issue*, winter/spring 1991, plate 7 and pages 74-75.

"Cenote" by Monica Mansour, as well as original poems by Kyra Galván, Elena Milán, Coral Bracho and Tomasa Rivera, with translations by Zoë Anglesey, will appear in the bilingual anthology *Mouth to Mouth: Twelve Contemporary Mexican Women Poets*, edited by Forest Gander (Milkweed Editions, 1993).

Roberto Obregón was a prize-winning Guatemalen poet who was assassinated by the military in 1972. "Equal to a Pebble" comes from *El Fuego Perdido*, Guatemala, 1971.

The Tule River—Olivia Silva's painting *El Río Tule* hangs in the El Centro de la Raza Gallery. She spent a month in-residence teaching painting at El Centro de la Raza in 1991. She was born in Solentiname, Nicaragua and began painting at age forty with encouragement from Ernesto Cardenal who initiated the painting collectives on that island. In her mid-sixties, she presently lives in Managua.

Francisco "Chico" Mendez, union leader for rubber workers and advocate for preserving the environment and indigenous human rights, was assassinated on December 22, 1988 in his home village of Xapuri in Acre, a northeastern state of Brazil.

Gabriel Morales was born in Yakima in 1960. He had an exhibit of his art in the El Centro de la Raza Gallery spring 1992. He participated in activities at El Centro de la Raza as a young man. He now lives in California.

Alfredo Arreguín has been commissioned by El Centro de la Raza to paint a work in commemoration of their 20th Anniversary. This work will be available to the public as a poster. He also contributed a painting for the Washington State Centennial Poster and has been exhibited and collected nationally and internationally, including by the Smithsonian Institute. He has provided book jacket paintings for *Lover of Horses* and *Amplitude*, by Tess Gallagher, and *Passage to the Waterfall* and *No Heroics Please: Uncollected Writings* by Raymond Carver.

Ray Gonzalez, poet, critic and translator, is Literature Director at the Guadalupe Cultural Arts Center in San Antonio, Texas. He is editor of *After Azatlan: Latino Poets of the Nineties* (David R. Bodine Publishers, 1992) and *Without Discovery A Native Response to Columbus: Essays by Native American and Chicano Writers* (Broken Moon Press, 1992).

EDITOR'S BIOGRAPHICAL NOTE

Zoë Anglesey picked fruit as an unpaid child laborer in Oregon. In an orphanage, she read her first newspapers meant to catch potato peelings during kitchen duty. These newspapers fed her curiosity about a world beyond the Willamette Valley. She first saw the insides of a college during a Christmas party inviting girls from the Children's Farm Home. It was here that she won an award for a poetry recitation at age ten. She finished high school in Aberdeen and college in Ellensburg, Washington. She has a Master's Degree in Creative Writing from New York University.

Having bypassed her desire to become a painter because she could not afford art school, and with her family already started, she took a teaching assignment in Yakima, Washington. She noticed that one of her students seemed to be perpetually tired. She visited Miguel's home which was a "farm" within the city limits. Anglesey learned that before school Miguel had already put in a shift tending chickens, pigs and goats. When she began to speak to him in her self-taught Spanish, he suddenly sparked as a student. She often took dictation from those in her class who, she was informed, were "retarded." Later she was chastised for giving her students from a variety of heritages their first A's and B's.

Anglesey organized grape and lettuce boycotts at a local super-market in Amherst, Massachusetts. In 1968 destined for Guatemala, she drove with husband and daughters throughout Mexico, and returned again in 1970 and 1972. Each trip she learned a bit more about United States history—from the Mexican point of view, as so vividly depicted in wall panels at the History Museum in Mexico City. She also searched out the murals by Diego Rivera and other Mexican painters—to "read."

In Guatemala she saw the impact of the war that began with Alvarado's military subjugation of the Mayan nations and how it was tragically prolonged after the 1954 U.S.-C.I.A. sponsored coup against the democratically elected government of Arbenz through the 1980s to the present. Passed like secret messages from hand to hand, she received gifts of folded poems by forbidden poets. People pulled out poetry books from behind secret panels by the guerrillero poets Otto René Castillo and Roberto Obregón. In 1972, after these experiences and many more, she translated and presented the poetry by these prize-winning poets.

The following year for International Women's Day, she organized and broadcast a tribute to Lolita Lebrón, the imprisoned Puerto Rican Nationalist. At this time she became familiar with Caribbean poetry appearing in anthologies edited by Jamaican poet Andrew Salkey, and in *Caliban*, edited by Roberto Márquez. Because she eventually translated some Caribbean poetry, she was invited to the Dominican Republic Writer's Union Conference in 1986. Between 1968 and 1988, she made ten trips to Central America, returning with poetry and poets in order to reveal the conditions imposed by war. Anglesey is the only U.S. person, as poet and translator, to have been invited to the Central American Writers Conferences held biannually from 1982 to 1988.

In New York she first read poetry at the Nuyorican Poets Cafe founded by Miguel Algarín whose brotherly embrace she enjoys to this day. She organized Central American poetry readings for Artists Call in New York at the height of the wars in El Salvador and against Nicaragua. For one such reading when Ernesto Cardenal participated, people started lining up around the Cooper Union block two hours early.

Anglesey's first book of poems is titled *Something More Than Force: Poems for Guatemala—1971-1982* (Adastra Press, 1983). She edited *Ixok Amar.go: Central American Women's Poetry for Peace* (out-of-print) a multilingual anthology in a bilingual format which collects poetry by women between the ages of eighty-six and sixteen. She edited the only bilingual book of contemporary U.S. women's poetry available to Central

American readers, published in Tegucigalpa, Honduras and featuring multicultural poets, which was translated by the Costa Rican poet Rodolfo "Popo" Dada. Forthcoming books feature jazz including her short story collection titled *Jam*. Anglesey is compiling and editing *New Fire: Jazz Musicians of the Nineties* with interviews, biographies and photographs.

Zoë Anglesey lived in Loisaida—the Puerto Rican Lower East Side of Manhattan—for over thirteen years. In New York she taught at West Side High School, Rikers Island Prison and at Boricua College. In Seattle 1990-1992, besides conducting poetry workshops at El Centro de la Raza, she teaches writing classes at Seattle Central Community College.